MW00657996

WELCOME TO THE WONDERFUL WORLD OF ECK!

MAHANTA

This book has been authored by and published under the supervision of the Mahanta, the Living ECK Master, Sri Harold Klemp. It is the Word of ECK.

WELCOME TO THE WONDERFUL WORLD OF ECK!

Your Membership Guidebook

Harold Klemp

ECKANKAR
Minneapolis
www.Eckankar.org

Welcome to the Wonderful World of ECK! Your Membership Guidebook

Printed in USA
ISBN: 978-1-57043-238-5
LCCN: 2006939877

Compiled by Sharon Kunin and Alison Powers

Edited by Patrick Carroll, Joan Klemp, and Anthony Moore

Cover art by Don McFadden

Cover design by Stan Burgess

Illustrations by Joe D. Bellows, Signy Cohen, Roy Kerswill, Fraser MacDonald, April Munson, Valerie Taglieri, and Ronald Wennekes

Photographs by Gordon Augustson, Stan Burgess, Art Galbraith, Robert Huntley, and Suzanne Percoskie

Second edition—2016

♾ This paper meets the requirements of ANSI/NISO Z39.48-1992 (Permanence of Paper).

Contents

Welcome

This guidebook to the joys and benefits of ECK membership is to help you get the most from your new life on the path of ECK.

To make it easy for you, this book features the most frequently asked questions of newer ECKists and my answers to them, listed by topic. For some questions I refer you to information and resources from Youth and Family Services, Membership Services, and other areas.

Though you may enjoy paging through this book in one sitting, it's designed as a quick reference you can pull off the shelf when a question presents itself. Whether you have a question on how to study the ECK discourses or want to find out what happens during an ECK initiation, this guidebook will serve you well.

A new world awaits you.

A new world awaits you. Be willing to put a little time and effort and a lot of heart into the ECK teachings.

With much joy, I welcome you to the wonderful world of ECK!

Harold

1

The Mahanta, the Living ECK Master

Sri Harold Klemp

1
The Mahanta, the Living ECK Master

What is the Master's main job?

Some of my talks and writings are instructive, where I give actual rules: Do this or that if you want to accomplish this or that. But many of the talks are purely for inspiration. Because as Soul, you have the God-knowledge within you.

My main job is to awaken the knowledge and love for the divine things that are already in your heart.

My main job is to awaken the knowledge and love for the divine things that are already in your heart. You are Soul. You are a child of God.

And your spiritual destiny is to become a Co-worker with God, to spread divine love to all those around you.

What is the meaning of the two sides of the Master?

The two sides of the Master are the Outer Master and the Inner Master.

The Inner Master is there, working when you sleep, or pray, or meditate, or contemplate. And the Outer Master is out here to provide the books, discourses, talks, and things of this nature. But the Outer and Inner Master are not two separate things—they're just two different aspects of one being who serves the Holy Spirit.

When will I meet the Master?

Your first meeting with the Mahanta, the Living ECK Master can take place in your dreams or in the waking state. It is indeed a blessed moment. An inner connection between you and the Mahanta begins to develop then, a connection that is vital to your spiritual growth. Even if you never meet the Living ECK Master in his outer form, you are always together inwardly.

How does the Mahanta work with everyone at once?

If you're in agreement with these principles of Divine Spirit, there is a bond between us, a connection.

In the inner self, I can be with all people in all places around the world. But only if they are in agreement with the principles of ECK. If you're in agreement with these principles of Divine Spirit, there is a bond between us, a connection.

In his physical body, the Mahanta, the Living ECK Master is like everyone else and can only be in one place at a time. In the Soul body, however, he is like the air that you breathe. He is everywhere. As the ECK, he can easily be with you and thousands of others in the very same moment.

To put it another way, you can think of the Inner Master, the Mahanta, as a body and yourself as one tiny cell within his body. Millions of other cells are in it too. The Mahanta is always with all the cells within his body, whether they are in his toe or in his head.

As the Mahanta, Divine Spirit, or the ECK, is able to work with you on a one-to-one basis. It can work with you with your strengths, it can work with you in your weaknesses, and it can help you just like a tutor.

The Mahanta is able to work with you on a one-to-one basis.

Sometimes standing behind your desk, sometimes working with you at the desk. Then sometimes just being with you. Being with you at work, on a walk, in rush-hour traffic. This is what the Mahanta, the Inner Master, can do and does.

What is the Darshan?

One form of the Darshan is the Gaze of the Master which has the power to uplift and heal all things.

There are two parts of the Darshan: meeting with the Master outwardly and being recognized by him, and meeting with him inwardly and traveling with him; seeing and being seen by him, and the enlightenment which comes with this act.

This is the gaze of love, this gaze that gives the love of God to people.

Does the Mahanta help me with my mission in this life?

Each individual is special, a spark of God, and has the ability to someday gain the consciousness of God—not to become God, but to gain God Consciousness or God-Realization.

First we develop Self-Realization: to know who and what we are and what our mission in this life may be.

First we develop Self-Realization. This is the self-recognition of truth: to know who and what we are and what our mission in this life may be. When we have achieved this state of consciousness, then our next goal is God-Realization and reaching the kingdom of heaven in this lifetime.

On every plane in the lower worlds, the Mahanta, the Living ECK Master works and operates to lift Soul to Its heritage of God Consciousness.

* * *

Autobiography of a Modern Prophet is my own story about the climb up the Mountain of God and attainment of God Consciousness. "Additional Study Aids," pages 97–100, lets you know where this and other ECKANKAR books may be requested.

Where can I get answers to my questions about life, love, and God?

The Easy Way technique is an opportunity in learning to rely on the Inner Master. Mentally ask your question while you're doing the Easy Way technique, and again ask it before dropping off to sleep at night. The answer will come, sometimes in an obvious manner. Other times it comes subtly—through the advice of a friend, a humorous anecdote, or as a symbolic dream that you develop the knack of interpreting for yourself.

List all your questions on a sheet of paper. A month later, review them to see if any have resolved themselves. Do this with all your questions every month, and send a report to me, if you like, regarding the results.

Look under "This Month's Exercise" in lesson 1 of *The Easy Way Discourses* for "The Easy Way" spiritual exercise. Later, you can adapt the technique of asking the Inner Master a question to other spiritual exercises as well.

Can I contact the Living ECK Master?

If you want to write a letter occasionally, please do. I read many of these physically. I read all of them as the Inner Master.

When you write your letter, you're basically opening yourself up to the Inner Master and saying, "I've put my troubles down in front of me. I recognize these as problems, and I would like something to be done about them unless it's karma that is necessary to work off for my own spiritual unfoldment. Then I will accept that too." This is how you go about it.

At times you may think you need to meet the Living ECK Master personally or speak with me by telephone. You may want to ask questions about your spiritual or physical life. But as you learn to place your attention on the Inner Master, the Mahanta will provide the answers you need.

As you learn to place your attention on the Inner Master, the Mahanta will provide the answers you need.

How does the Mahanta help me resolve karma?

When someone first comes to the path of ECK, the Mahanta, the Living ECK Master takes over the karma for this individual. He arranges it, puts it in neat little rows, and then gives it back.

People must pay their own debts. They must

reap their own rewards. I can't do that for them. No one can do it for them. In ECK, we don't have the concept of a savior, because we're not saving anybody from anything—unless we're helping people save themselves from themselves.

This is what karma is: doing it to yourself, and then complaining about others doing it to you.

One of the benefits of putting your spiritual life in the hands of the Mahanta is that much of your karma can be worked off in the dream state.

With this help from the Master, all of your karma can be resolved in this lifetime. You will be free of the wheel of reincarnation.

How does the Outer Master give spiritual help?

Some ways are the ECK discourses, books, seminar talks, and publications like the *Mystic World*.

The *Mystic World* is my personal newsletter to you. Four times a year, this four-color, eight-page periodical comes to the home of every current member of ECKANKAR. It clarifies many things in the works of ECK to help each Soul reach God.

I write from my heart with your spiritual needs in mind.

I write from my heart with your spiritual needs in mind, be it my feature articles, Wisdom Notes, or answers to your questions in the "Ask the Master" columns. In each issue you'll also find information on any new books, spiritual programs, or other aids I've prepared to help ease your climb up the spiritual mountain.

In each issue you'll find aids I've prepared to help ease your climb up the spiritual mountain.

There's also news from major ECK seminars and letters from ECKists about dreams, their spiritual experiences, and other insights they've received in their ECK studies.

Many areas of the world hold *Mystic World* discussion classes, where ECKists meet to share their insights on what I've written in the current issue.

2

ECK Discourse Study Tips

2
ECK Discourse Study Tips

The ECK discourses are letters either I or Paul Twitchell[1] have written to explain different facets of ECKANKAR and the spiritual life—how to live it. They include some of the more interesting things about the spiritual techniques, places to go and things to do, but mainly what you can do to help yourself spiritually to make this a worthwhile lifetime.

They include many spiritual techniques. These methods are a step-by-step, month-by-month plan that breaks up old, ingrained thought patterns that act like chains upon your hands and feet.

Each monthly lesson offers you a new measure of spiritual freedom.

Each monthly lesson offers you a new measure of spiritual freedom.

How can I get the most out of my discourse study?

The discourses are written with a secret, internal rhythm that gradually unfolds your consciousness in a very precise and orderly manner. To help you stay in this rhythm, read lesson 1 the month your new discourse arrives. Then study

1. Paul Twitchell was the modern-day founder of ECKANKAR.

just one new lesson per month. You're welcome to review past lessons at any time.

You may share your discourse with your family if you like. You will find a list of the ECK discourses at the end of this chapter.

The following study tips can help you open to the secret melody within every discourse.

The following study tips can help you open to the secret melody of divine love, wisdom, and understanding within every discourse.

- First, get an overview by reading the entire lesson. Underline or highlight important sentences, and make notes in the margin if you like.
- Practice the spiritual exercise given at the end of the lesson.
- Look over the workbook activities for the month's lesson.
- Use the workbook activities to focus on one or two sections each week. You will be more aware of your spiritual experiences.
- At the end of the month, you can review the entire lesson for a new overview of the topic.

Then go on to the next lesson. It's not important to feel that you've mastered the monthly spiritual exercise. Doing them on a daily basis naturally opens the door to the Light and Sound of God in ways that are just right for you.

When can I start taking advanced discourses?

After two years of exploring the teachings of ECK as a member, you will receive an invitation to request the Second Initiation in ECK. You'll find more on this in chapter 8.

The Second Initiation qualifies you to receive advanced discourses and special inner and outer training to move toward your first spiritual goal of Self-Realization. Each year of discourses gives Soul new experiences in the Light and Sound of God. The Second Initiation opens Soul to receive this greater wisdom, love, and freedom.

The Second Initiation qualifies you to receive advanced discourses and special inner and outer training.

What do I do if I've fallen behind in my personal discourse study?

It's important to keep current with your ECK discourses, studying one new chapter each month. If you fall behind, study the current month's lesson. Watch for a key point for reflection. Put your attention on that one passage or idea, keeping your heart open and the mind out of it. Listen to the Mahanta, the Inner Master, speak to your heart about the secret meaning of the passage. Then skim one or two past discourses too. Catch what you can and move on.

What are the titles and sequence of the ECK discourses?

A description of each discourse series can be found in *Your Road Map to the ECK Teachings* (See "Additional Study Aids" in the back of this book).

The Easy Way Discourses
The ECK Dream 1 Discourses
The ECK Dream 2 Discourses

Advanced Discourses

Letters of Light & Sound 1
Letters of Light & Sound 2
Soul Travel 1—The Illuminated Way

Soul Travel 2
The Secret Way
The Precepts of ECKANKAR
The ECK Satsang Discourses, First Series
The ECK Satsang Discourses, Second Series
The ECK Satsang Discourses, Third Series
The ECK Satsang Discourses, Fourth Series
The Master 1 Discourses
The Master 2 Discourses
The Master 3 Discourses
The Master 4 Discourses

3

Tips for Spiritual Exercises and Dream Study

3
Tips for Spiritual Exercises and Dream Study

Tips for Spiritual Exercises

How do the spiritual exercises help me?

When you start to do the Spiritual Exercises of ECK, the Light and Sound of the Holy Spirit begin to enter you through an invisible communication line, and changes come about in your personality. You become a more independent, thoughtful, self-motivated individual because you are taking the first steps toward self-mastery. And self-mastery means that you are in charge of yourself.

You become a more independent, thoughtful, self-motivated individual because you are taking the first steps toward self-mastery.

You will find that your connection with the Inner Master and the ECK grows stronger with the practice of the Spiritual Exercises of ECK. Day by day, you will realize more clearly the love of the Mahanta for each Soul in the worlds of God. In time you will understand that you no longer walk alone, for the Inner Master serves as your constant guide and companion.

What is the difference between meditation and contemplation?

Contemplation is a method that enables you to begin to actively explore the inner worlds of your own being. It is different than meditation, a passive state in which the practitioner goes within and just quietly waits for the light.

The spiritual exercises work similarly to physical exercises. If you want your body to be strong and healthy, you've got to swim or run or do something to keep fit. For the Soul body, we do the Spiritual Exercises of ECK, a form of inner communication.

Soul is an active, happy being. Meditation slows the spiritual process.

When should I do my spiritual exercises?

I always recommend that people do their spiritual exercises every day. But they should be done with a sense of excitement and anticipation.

Try setting a specific time and place for this daily appointment with the Holy Spirit.

If you practice the spiritual exercises on a regular schedule, like a meal, you'll get the inner nourishment you seek. Try setting a specific time and place for this daily appointment with the Holy Spirit.

How do I know if I'm doing the spiritual exercises correctly?

If you eat the same food every day for two weeks, it can get pretty dull. You may enjoy it the first day, and the second day is all right. But by the second week, you're tired of it. So you experiment; you experiment with something new.

It's the same with the spiritual exercises. You experiment with them; you try new things. You're in your own God Worlds. I've gone to different extremes with the exercises, trying very complicated ones I developed for myself, dropping them when they didn't work anymore.

It's like a vein of gold running through a mountain. You're on it for a while, then the vein runs out and you have to scout around and find another one.

Are we learning something new every day from what we're doing? Are we getting insight and help from the inner? This is what we ought to be working for.

How do I keep my mind from wandering off during contemplation?

Paul Twitchell, the modern-day founder of ECKANKAR, once wrote that the mind likes to jump around like a monkey.

First of all, don't worry about it.

Second, entertain your mind during the Spiritual Exercises of ECK. Do an exercise a slightly different way each time. Let the mind play. Remember who is watching your mind play: the real you (Soul). Come to that realization during your spiritual exercise, and you will realize that Soul Itself is calm and doesn't jump around.

It's hard to get the mind absolutely still. But by suddenly knowing that you, the watcher (Soul), are still, the antics of the mind won't upset you anymore.

Remember who is watching your mind play: the real you (Soul). By suddenly knowing that you, the watcher (Soul), are still, the antics of the mind won't upset you anymore.

Tips for Dream Study

How can studying my dreams help me?

Dreams are like a daily report card. They show how you are doing in your spiritual mission, even if you don't know you have one. Dreams tell how you are getting on in your relationship with God and life.

There is a spiritual side to every experience or event, no matter how large or small.

There is a spiritual side to every experience or event, no matter how large or small, and whether or not it occurs in everyday life or in a dream.

I wish I could remember my dreams better. Can you help?

Some people naturally enjoy vivid recollections of their dream state, but those who don't can develop the skill.

You can set a dream in your mind before you wake up by repeating the main points of it, then talking about it out loud or writing it down as soon as you wake up.

It is also possible to develop a sharper recall of the dream state by keeping a notebook by the bed, with pen and light at hand. Make a resolution to wake—even in the middle of the night—to record any memory of the dream state, no matter how trivial it seems.

Does each dream have a spiritual meaning or lesson involved? Or are some just purely creations of my imagination?

Every experience, waking or dream, has a lesson or message to impart to us. But let the meanings of your inner and outer experiences come naturally. In other words, if the lesson or message isn't clear, don't force it.

Soul, the spiritual self that you are, will send another dream in some other way until your human self can easily grasp the meaning.

Accept each dream as a spiritual gift.

In ECKANKAR, dream study works on all levels. As with all things of a divine nature, accept each dream as a spiritual gift. Wonder about it. Roll it gently around in your mind to see whether loving patience on your part will reveal its significance.

This approach is the reason the ECKANKAR spiritual studies are called the Easy Way.

One other point.

Dream experiences are real experiences from another time, place, or dimension. Some of them are from past lives, which you'd expect to be straightforward. Yet here's where the mind—or what you call "just purely creations of my imagination"—comes in.

The dream censor is a function, or part, of the mind. For purely karmic reasons it may decide that a certain past life would be too much of a shock to you. You might break off a relationship. Yet that relationship in the present time may be necessary to bring an important insight to you.

So the dream censor tones down dreams. It

lets a dreamer go ahead with life and so profit from past-life experiences.

* * *

If you want to know more about remembering, understanding, and interpreting your dreams, read *The Art of Spiritual Dreaming* (also an audiobook). "Additional Study Aids," at the back of this book, lets you know where this and other ECKANKAR books may be requested.

4

ECK Satsang Classes
(Group Discourse Study)

4
ECK Satsang Classes
(Group Discourse Study)

What is an ECK Satsang class?

Satsang class is a spiritual forum for ECK members led by an Arahata (a teacher of ECK classes) to explore the ECK discourses together. The size of the class is usually from three to twelve members.

In class, you will be exploring a lesson you've already studied.

What's in it for me?

The Satsang class is a spiritual laboratory. It is a place where chelas (spiritual students), new and old, are invited to explore a wide range of ECK ideas. The purpose of Satsang is to help each person find his or her own relationship with Spirit.

The purpose of Satsang is to help each person find his or her own relationship with Spirit.

Satsang offers you the opportunity to hear the ECK speak in a personal way to you and to others in the class.

You can share experiences, ask questions, and learn ways to find your own answers.

One of the benefits of being in ECKANKAR is simply being with a group of people who have had experiences in life that are not ordinary or commonplace. Experiences with the Light and Sound of ECK.

You've become familiar with experiences and insights into life that the average person does not have.

You've become familiar with a lot of different experiences and have insights into life that the average person does not have. And so you can talk about things with each other that people outside of ECK would consider on the far side. But these are some of the facts of life.

Through these shared experiences and insights, you'll gain a broader viewpoint to recognize your own success with Soul Travel, dreams, and the Spiritual Exercises of ECK. You can realize the many ways the Mahanta, the Inner Master gives you guidance and how each discourse lesson relates to you and your life today.

And most of all, the Satsang class will help you share the Mahanta's love for you as Soul—a love greater than words can express.

How do I join a Satsang class?

For information on how to join a Satsang class, check your local ECK newsletter or call your ECK center or class coordinator.

Tell him or her you are a new ECK member and would like to join a Satsang class. Ask if there's one open or if it's possible to get one started in your area.

You can also ask to visit a class one time and experience what it's like.

You can ask to visit a class one time and experience what it's like.

If you do not know who to contact in your area, call or write Membership Services at the ECKANKAR Spiritual Center, (952) 380-2222, Monday through Friday, 8:00 a.m.–5:00 p.m., central time.

Reading the ECK discourses and making contact with the ECK Sound Current is also Satsang. If you study alone, the workbook activities and audio excerpts will help you delve more deeply into the discourse lessons.

5

Youth Classes and Study Materials

5
Youth Classes and Study Materials

Each Soul who comes into a family is different. One child may need only a brief explanation of the ECK principles. He acts like he is being reminded of things he already knows. Another may need a full introduction to these brand-new ideas. He seems to gradually open his eyes to a world of spiritual truth as you watch.

Every child has his own special link with the Divine.

Every child has his own special link with the Divine.

Are there ECK discourses for youth?

Yes. The ECK youth study books were written to help answer questions about life and give spiritual education. They are for youth aged three through seventeen.

Each study book has twelve lessons written to address the spiritual opportunities and challenges facing youth today. At the end of each month's lesson are exercises and activities to explore the spiritual topics even further.

Many adults also enjoy the simple clarity of the youth study books and read them to supplement their own ECK studies.

Is there an ECK publication for youth?

Letter of Light is especially for youth. This four-color, four-page newsletter is packed with personal stories and spiritual experiences, games and photos from young ECKists around the world.

Letter of Light *contains a special column where I answer questions from youth.*

Each issue also contains a special column where I answer questions from youth. Topics range from ways to handle peer pressure and conflicts with friends and family to help in understanding dreams and discovering your spiritual mission in this life.

Youth of all ages will enjoy this fun-filled newsletter.

Anyone may subscribe to the Letter of Light. *Call or write the ECKANKAR Spiritual Center to do so.*

Another resource is the book *Youth Ask a Modern Prophet about Life, Love, and God*. This book is a compilation of twenty years of questions from youth around the world and my answers to them as the Mahanta, the Living ECK Master.

The following section, from Youth and Family Services at the ECKANKAR Spiritual Center, answers key questions about youth activities.

Youth and Family Services Answers Your Frequently Asked Questions

Does my child need to start from the beginning of the youth-study-book series?

No, you can begin with the book most suited to your child's level of understanding. Unlike the adult discourses, no ECK youth study book is a prerequisite for another. They are separate from ECK membership and are purchased as books.

At age eighteen a young adult member can begin study of the adult discourses, starting with *The Easy Way Discourses*.

Are there youth Satsang classes too?

Youth Satsang classes offer a unique spiritual forum for youth to share their experiences and learn from each other.

There are! Youth Satsang classes offer a unique spiritual forum for youth to share their experiences and learn from each other.

If you would like to find out about

youth Satsang classes in your area, and you don't know how to reach the local ECK class coordinator or the Youth and Family Program director, contact your Regional ECK Spiritual Aide (RESA). Let him or her know you are a new ECK member and would like your children to attend a Satsang class. "Additional Study Aids," at the back of this book, lets you know how to contact your RESA.

All of the youth study materials, including the study books, are available to interested newcomers.

Can youth who aren't ECK members study the youth study books and attend a youth Satsang class?

With a completed permission form from their parents, they are welcome to attend.

All of the youth study materials, including the study books, are available to interested newcomers for purchase.

What can I do if there aren't enough youth in my area to have a Satsang class?

If it is not possible for a youth to be in a Satsang class, parents can still provide the Satsang experience. A Satsang can be any spiritual gathering in the name of the ECK.

Families are encouraged to study ECK together. The important thing is that youth have the opportunity to live in the Light and Sound of God by putting their attention on the Mahanta and the ECK teachings.

The important thing is that youth have the opportunity to live in the Light and Sound of God.

The booklet *Your Children and the ECK Discourses—Handbook for ECK Parents,* by Paul Twitchell, is filled with suggestions and ideas for parents to help their children get the most out of their ECK studies and foster a strong connection with the Mahanta. You can request the booklet from the ECKANKAR Spiritual Center. "Additional Study Aids," at the back of this book, lets you know how.

What ECK activities are available for youth?

Many regions offer the following for youth and families:

- ECK youth Satsang classes
- ECK Worship Services
- ECK major and regional seminars with youth programs
- ECK youth book discussion classes
- Youth *Letter of Light* discussion classes

- ECK youth forums
  These are small, open discussions on spiritual topics in ECK, open to youth under eighteen.
- ECK family campouts
- ECK leadership and service opportunities
- ECKANKAR Religious Emblem Program for Scouts

ECK youth forums are open discussions on spiritual topics, open to youth under eighteen.

Here's how to find out more about these ECK youth activities in your area.

Contact the Youth and Family Program director, if you know who that is, or your Regional ECK Spiritual Aide (RESA). "Additional Study Aids," at the back of this book, lets you know how to contact your RESA.

You can also request a free study-materials booklet from the ECKANKAR Spiritual Center. It lists all the study materials available for youth and adults.

6

Major ECKANKAR Seminars in Minneapolis, Minnesota

6
Major ECKANKAR Seminars
in Minneapolis, Minnesota

Why are ECK seminars important?

An ECK seminar is always a spiritual occasion. It stirs and speeds up the spiritual activity within Soul. This is why it's important to come to the seminars when you can. We have a number of workshops, roundtables, and talks designed to help you learn how to live the life of ECK.

An ECK seminar stirs and speeds up the spiritual activity within Soul.

An ECK seminar is a celebration of like-minded people, each taking the next step in their spiritual journey.

What's it like at a major ECKANKAR seminar?

The heart of the seminar experience is feeling the divine love that comes through on an occasion such as this. The ECK flow is stronger than usual when we all get together. You can then carry some of this love home with you after the weekend is over.

I have always found it a great privilege to attend the ECK seminars. There was a time that I loved to sit in the audience and just soak up everything. Each talk gave me a little greater understanding.

I have always found it a great privilege to attend the ECK seminars. Each talk gave me greater understanding.

The following special note, from Seminar Services at the ECKANKAR Spiritual Center, gives helpful information about the major ECKANKAR seminars.

A Special Note from Seminar Services

You are invited to come and see the Mahanta, the Living ECK Master speak in person.

This is an opportunity to step into the sacred moment when the Godman of the age addresses all life with the divine

message. In his words and in his presence is a special message just for you, and a wondrous gift of love.

And if you cannot attend in person, your seminar weekend can be a pilgrimage of the heart—no less a step into a larger room of living.

This pilgrimage is a time of deep spiritual renewal. It is a special time to experience the Darshan both outwardly and inwardly in the heightened awareness that an ECK seminar brings.

It is a special time to experience the Darshan both outwardly and inwardly in the heightened awareness that an ECK seminar brings.

The ECK Springtime Seminar is usually in April, and the ECK Worldwide Seminar is in October, near or on the date of the ECK Spiritual New Year.[1] An invitation flyer is sent to ECK members before each seminar.

Seminars include inspiring talks, workshops, group HU songs, creative arts, youth programs, fellowship, music, and much, much more!

Go to the ECKANKAR Web site (**www.Eckankar.org**) and click "Upcoming Seminars." You'll find a wealth of helpful seminar details: dates, location, preregistration, housing reservations, sign-up to hear the Master's talk through the Internet, Temple of ECK visitor information, and more.

1. See chapter 11, "The Traditions of ECK," for more about the ECK Spiritual New Year.

7

The Four ECK Celebrations of Life

7
The Four ECK Celebrations of Life

These four ECK ceremonies celebrate Soul's journey through life.

They are at the heart of the activities of mankind. In one form or another, this has been the basis for what people do. As they go through life, they naturally enter these stages and there is some kind of rite or celebration to help them.

Each stage is a rite of passage, a way of coming into being.

ECK clerics (ministers) perform the ECK Consecration Ceremony, the ECK Rite of Passage, the ECK Wedding Ceremony, and the ECK Memorial Service.

We welcome Soul into this world with the ECK Consecration Ceremony.

- **The ECK Consecration Ceremony**

  We welcome Soul into this world with the ECK Consecration Ceremony.

  This beautiful ECK ceremony blesses the entrance of the child into the ECK teachings in this lifetime. It allows family and friends to come together to dedicate themselves to leading the child in the ways of Divine Spirit.

The ECK Consecration Ceremony celebrates new life and the beginning of a new phase in Soul's journey home to God. It also celebrates the commitment of the parents to bring a spiritual awareness into the home and the life of the child. It is for infants and very young children. Older children can also have the service, but someone nearing age thirteen instead prepares for the ECK Rite of Passage.

Consecration *means to declare sacred. It is dedicating yourself and all you do, say, think, and feel to God.*

Consecration means to declare sacred. It is dedicating yourself and all you do, say, think, and feel to God.

- **The ECK Rite of Passage**

With the ECK Rite of Passage, we celebrate the stage of life which begins as the child enters the threshold of adulthood, around age thirteen, but one may take it to perhaps age twenty-one.

This ceremony celebrates the youth's personal commitment to the ECK teachings and growing awareness of his or her true spiritual nature.

The ECK Rite of Passage normally follows a preliminary meeting by a member of the ECK clergy with the youth and parent(s) and often a period of spiritual training for the youth. Some areas offer spiritual training classes for the youth in preparation for the ceremony.

A special guidebook, *The ECK Rite of Passage Youth Study Guide*, is available to help young ECKists prepare for this unique ceremony. For information on how to get a copy, see "Additional Study Aids" in the back of this book.

- **The ECK Wedding Ceremony**

We celebrate marriage with the ECK Wedding Ceremony.

This celebration of life occurs when we find our complement in another person. When two people come together with pure hearts, their marriage is filled with the ECK (Holy Spirit).

When two people come together with pure hearts, their marriage is filled with the ECK (Holy Spirit).

This lovely wedding ceremony establishes this bond between two people, setting them firmly on the path toward greater mutual understanding and love.

- **The ECK Memorial Service**

This ceremony honors Soul's departure from the physical plane to continue life in the God Worlds of ECK.

When a loved one translates into a higher realm of existence, leaving the physical realm behind, it's a time for those who remain to honor this Soul's continuation, to celebrate eternal spiritual life.

We celebrate the continuity of life with the ECK Memorial Service. This ceremony celebrates life and the presence of the Mahanta at all levels of existence.

Can I know what's in each ceremony?

There is a booklet for each of the four celebrations of life that includes the complete ceremony. You can receive copies from the ECKANKAR Spiritual Center at a modest cost. "Additional Study Aids," at the back of this book, lets you know how.

8

The ECK Initiations

8
The ECK Initiations

The teachings of ECK offer a whole new world to the individual who wants to find God. And the ECK initiations are among your most valuable aids on this direct path to God.

An ECK initiation is a spiritual rite that brings you closer to the Holy Spirit.

What is an ECK initiation?

It is simply a spiritual rite that brings you closer to ECK, the Holy Spirit. There is no use of water, as in baptism. Nor a laying on of hands. Rather, the aspirant meets with an ECK Initiator,[1] to whom the Mahanta gives the power to carry out this sacred trust.

When Soul comes out of the initiation, the individual may or may not have a conscious awareness of what transpired on the inner planes. Nevertheless, the Light and Sound of God has put a greater light to Soul than ever before.

This is why the Mahanta is called the Light Giver. Soul is given a greater amount of the Light and Sound of the Holy Spirit.

1. Chapter 9 explains ECK Initiators.

How will the initiation help me in my daily life?

The ECK initiation is a spiritual awakening.

It will awaken in you a desire to give more love, service, and goodwill to everyone who enters the sphere of your new state of awareness.

You find a greater ability to handle fear, guilt, and uncertainty. In their place come humility, a more grateful heart, courage, dignity, and joy.

You will find a greater ability to handle fear, guilt, and uncertainty. In their place come humility, a more grateful heart, courage, dignity, and joy.

How is the linkup made?

The Mahanta, not the Initiator, makes the actual linkup between Soul and ECK. In this regard, the Mahanta is the sole agent of God, for he is an Adept of the highest order—able to reach all levels of heaven. He is the Master of every universe. At home in the Far Country, he travels from the Physical Plane to the Ocean of Love and Mercy, and beyond. He has the wisdom and power to protect the neophyte in ECK, as well as any High Initiate.[2]

The Mahanta, the Living ECK Master holds the key to SUGMAD.

What about the First Initiation? When can I expect to get it, and how does it come?

The First Initiation takes place during your first year of study in the spiritual works of ECK, and the only witness is the Mahanta (the Inner Master), who performs it. It always occurs in the

2. A High Initiate is of the Fifth Circle of ECK Initiation or above.

dream state. The purpose of the ECK initiation is to give you a closer bond with Divine Spirit.

The First Initiation is the first real guidepost on one's journey home to God, the initial linkup between Soul and Divine Spirit.

The First Initiation is the first real guidepost on one's journey home to God, the initial linkup between Soul and Divine Spirit.

Three years of the ECK discourse study program are available to you as a First Initiate.

How can I remember my First Initiation if I don't recall my dreams?

Many people recall some part of the First Initiation, though others do not. Whatever the case, the Mahanta gives it to all during their first year of ECK study. This Dream Initiation occurs in a place you may visit again by singing *Alayi* (ah-LAH-yee) during a spiritual exercise. This word is for the physical plane.

If you sincerely want to learn about your Dream Initiation, sing this word daily for a month. Keep a dream journal. In the morning, allow an extra ten minutes in your schedule to jot down any impressions or dream memories, no matter how faint or silly.

Above all, be patient. Stick with this plan for a month. Soon you will catch a whole new outlook on the First Initiation and your relation to ECK.

When will I get the Second Initiation?

As you approach two years of study in the ECK discourses, the Living ECK Master will send you a special letter inviting you to request the Second Initiation.

How will I know if I'm ready to take the initiation?

At the Second Initiation, your karma is taken over by the Mahanta, the Living ECK Master and given back to you to work off in an orderly, forward-moving manner.

Sometimes the karma works off in the dream state.

The Master has sent you the pink slip for initiation. The gift has already been given, but the chela must accept it. You may take the initiation whenever you are willing.

What can I expect at the Second Initiation?

It's a short ceremony. It takes anywhere from half an hour to an hour.

In the outer rite, an Initiator gives you a secret word to sing during a spiritual exercise. The word fine-tunes you to the life stream of God, Divine Spirit, and is also for protection.

The inner half of the Second Initiation may occur before, during, or after the outer event, but it is the latter that counts as a valid initiation here. And each initiation is unique, though there is a similarity among those of the same circle.

Each initiation is unique, but you still have to put in your time. There are some things a book just can't teach you about living.

Can my family take the Second Initiation with me?

Yes. Family members living in your home may take the Second Initiation with you, whether they are members of ECKANKAR or not. Your children (through age 17) can share the Second Initiation with you, whether or not they attend the ceremony.

What about other ECK initiations?

After the Second, a period of four to six years or more is established between each initiation, and no one is to ask for an initiation beyond the Second. To do so stops one's spiritual growth, and it will not start again until the Master steps in.

You can be really smart in head knowledge, but you still have to put in your time. It has to be done, because there are some things a book just can't teach you about living. Until you have this seasoning, you really don't have the understanding and compassion that one needs as he goes higher and higher in the ECK circles of initiation.

Until you have this seasoning, you don't have the understanding and compassion one needs as he goes higher.

How can I learn more about initiations in ECK?

Sometime go to the indexes of *The Shariyat-Ki-Sugmad,* the holy book of ECK. Turn to the sections in the two volumes that relate to initiation, for the subject is well worth your time.

You can get an insight into what happens on the inner during the ECK initiation in *The Golden Heart,* Mahanta Transcripts, Book 4, pages 72–74. This information is also in audio recordings of my talk "The Rope of Karma."

Article 25, "The First ECK Initiations," in *The Living Word,* Book 2, is helpful too.

For an overview of the ECKANKAR spiritual program and the opportunities it brings you, see the time line on page 101. It gives an eagle-eyed view of the Master's outer help through each leg of your journey home to God.

"Additional Study Aids," at the back of this book, lets you know where to find ECKANKAR books and recordings.

9

ECKANKAR Clergy

9
ECKANKAR Clergy

How do you become an ECK cleric (minister)?

Both men and women, Fifth Initiates or above, can be ordained into the ECK clergy.

All have been chelas of ECKANKAR for twenty or more years during which they studied, faced, and lived the ECK works every day. That study is in-depth training in ECK theology. It is more schooling than most divinity students get. In addition, the study of ECK is very practical in that it relates directly to the heart of daily living—unlike a divinity school, which may offer students a sheltered life for years.

ECK clergy have been chelas of ECKANKAR for twenty or more years during which they studied, faced, and lived the ECK works every day.

The following information, from Spiritual Services, answers key questions about the ECK clergy.

Spiritual Services Answers Frequently Asked Questions

What does an ECK cleric do?

A cleric's duties include leading ECK Worship Services; wedding, consecration, and memorial services; and rites of passage. See chapter 7 for more about these four ECK celebrations of life.

An ECK cleric may also be appointed as an ECK Initiator and ECK Spiritual Aide.

What is an ECK Initiator?

The ECK Initiator is a member of the ECK clergy who has been appointed by the Living ECK Master to perform ECK initiation ceremonies. See chapter 8 for more information about ECK initiations.

What is an ECK Spiritual Aide (ESA) and an ESA session?

An ESA session, though not counseling, can help you find your own answers through Divine Spirit.

The ESA is a member of the ECK clergy, is an Initiator, and is also specially appointed by the Living ECK Master to meet with individuals who wish personal spiritual assistance.

An ESA session, though not counseling, can help you find your own answers in challenging situations through the personal guidance of Divine Spirit. It is of a sacred and confidential nature.

ESAs also lead roundtables on spiritual topics about the ECK teachings.

Are there fees for any of these services?

There are no fees for clergy services, but ECK clerics may accept donations to ECKANKAR.

There are no fees for clergy services, but ECK clerics may accept donations to ECKANKAR.

How can I meet with an ECK cleric, Initiator, or ESA?

If you don't know the Spiritual Services coordinator in your area, contact your Regional ECK Spiritual Aide (RESA). Let him or her know you are a new ECK member and what you'd like to know more about. "Additional Study Aids," at the back of this book, lets you know how to contact your RESA. You may also contact Spiritual Services at the ECKANKAR Spiritual Center for the name of an Initiator or ESA near you.

You can meet with an ECK Initiator or ESA at the major ECKANKAR seminars[1] in Minneapolis, Minnesota, and at most regional ECK seminars around the world. Just go to the seminar Spiritual Services desk. Prior appointments are not needed.

---

1. Chapter 6 explains the major ECKANKAR seminars.

10

The Temple of ECK and Spiritual Campus

10
The Temple of ECK and Spiritual Campus

What is the role of the Temple of ECK in Chanhassen, Minnesota?

The Temple of ECK is both a Golden Wisdom Temple and a local community church. It is a place for all people who love God and is the home of the ECK teachings in the physical plane.

The guardian of the Temple of ECK in Chanhassen is, of course, the Living ECK Master. The Temple is a gathering place for inner and outer study. Seekers of truth come here physically, in the dream state, in contemplation, and via Soul Travel to study the holy works of ECK.

Seekers of truth come here physically, in the dream state, in contemplation, and via Soul Travel.

ECK Worship Services are provided for the public and ECKists who choose to expand their states of consciousness. Introductory workshops and ECK classes, including Satsang classes, are also conducted here.

The Temple of ECK is the spiritual vortex on the physical plane from which the spiritual food of the teachings of ECK will come to feed those who hunger for God.

The Temple of ECK is thus in the service of God. It stands as a beacon of divine Light and love, for both you and the world—a gift to all.

The Temple of ECK stands as a beacon of divine Light and love, for both you and the world.

You can visit **www.Temple*of*ECK.org** and take a virtual tour.

If you want to know more about Golden Wisdom Temples, see the booklet *ECK Wisdom Temples, Spiritual Cities, & Guides: A Brief History.* "Additional Study Aids," at the back of this book, lets you know where to find this and other ECKANKAR books.

The following information, from Temple Services, answers key questions about the ECKANKAR Spiritual Center (ESC) and campus.

Temple Services Answers Your Questions

What is the ECKANKAR Spiritual Campus?

The campus includes the Temple of ECK, the ECK Celebrations of Life Chapel, the ECKANKAR Spiritual Center, and several miles of spiritual contemplation trails that reveal the beauty of the 174 acres of property. You can view the campus on ECKANKAR's Web site at **www.Temple*of*ECK.org**.

The campus stands at the crossroads of humanity's quest for spiritual freedom, at the spiritual center of the world. It is *your* spiritual campus. Visit it, walk the land and trails, come to the seminars in Minneapolis, renew yourself spiritually.

What is the ECKANKAR Spiritual Center?

The ECKANKAR Spiritual Center is the worldwide headquarters for the myriad activities of the ECK mission for the world. These activities include producing and mailing the ECK study materials and introductory packets, planning and preparing seminars, maintaining the official ECKANKAR Web site (**www.Eckankar.org**), and many other spiritual programs.

From this spiritual center the Mahanta, the Living ECK Master brings forth the eternal message of spiritual liberation.

From this spiritual center the Living Word—the Mahanta, the Living ECK Master—brings forth the eternal message of spiritual liberation to the world.

What is the purpose of the outdoor ECK Celebrations of Life Chapel?

The ECK Celebrations of Life Chapel is all about bringing more divine love into everything we do. Love grows with each consecration, rite of passage, wedding, and memorial service.

The outdoor chapel with its surrounding gardens is a wonderful place to contemplate and enjoy the sacred grounds.

The outdoor chapel with its surrounding gardens is a wonderful place to contemplate and enjoy the sacred grounds. Evening HU chants are sometimes held in the outdoor chapel during the summer months. You are warmly invited to come, sing *HU*, and celebrate life!

11

The Traditions of ECK

11
The Traditions of ECK

What are the Spiritual Years of ECK?

Each new spiritual year, which begins on October 22, carries a theme. This theme, or name, gives a focus to the spiritual direction and efforts of ECK initiates for the next twelve months.

Each new spiritual year carries a theme.

What are these themes?

The spiritual themes are shown in the following circle.

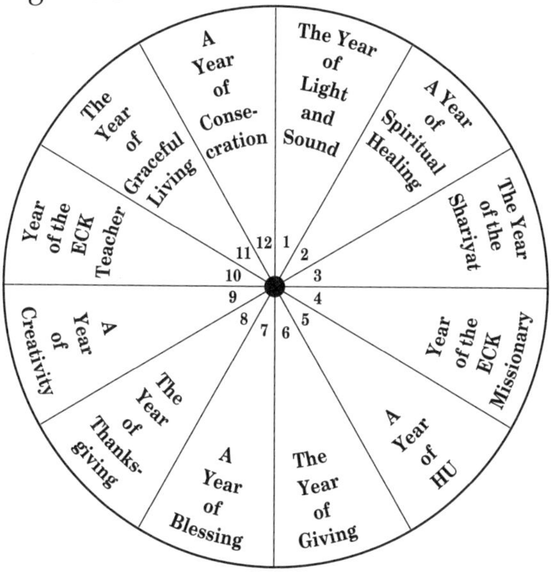

A Cosmic Sea of Words: The ECKANKAR Lexicon explains the focus and direction of each spiritual theme in detail; look under "Spiritual Years of ECK." You can also read more in article 38 of *The Living Word*, Book 3, "The Spiritual Years of ECK."

How can I know what spiritual year we're in right now?

See the diagram on page 75.

The cycle of twelve years is synchronized to run in order beginning on October 22, 2001.

The cycle of spiritual years begins with "The Year of Light and Sound."

The Spiritual New Year of ECK is a time of rededication.

What does the ECK Spiritual New Year signify?

October 22 marks the Spiritual New Year of ECK. Taking place in autumn, it signifies the high point or spiritual harvest in the year's cycle. It is a time of rededication.

The ECK Spiritual New Year also celebrates the birth date of Paul Twitchell, the modern-day founder of ECKANKAR. Of more spiritual import, however, is the fact that it was on this day that he accepted the Rod of ECK Power and became the Mahanta, the Living ECK Master.

He came to help people find their way home to God in the most direct way.

So the Spiritual New Year is the beginning of a new, higher cycle for the coming year. Historically, October 22 is the day that the Living ECK Master of the times receives the Rod of ECK Power and begins his spiritual duties.

How do ECKists celebrate ECKANKAR Founder's Day?

Founder's Day, another day that is gaining prominence in the ECK tradition, is September 17, the day Paul Twitchell translated from the physical plane. It is also a time of respect for him as a giver of the sacred Light and Sound. However, this quiet celebration is not intended to be a day of worship. An initiate may or may not choose to take part in the significance of this day.

What are Harji dinners?

Harji is an affectionate nickname for me, as Paulji was for Paul Twitchell.

These Harji dinners are actually a combined spiritual and social function in the ECK community. They are occasions for thanksgiving—a thankfulness for Soul's having earned the right to recognize and accept the ECK gospel in this lifetime.

The Harji dinner provides a setting where principles of ECK can be discussed with visitors in a light, informal way. It also bonds the ECK initiates together in their appreciation for each other.

The dinner provides a congenial setting of good food and company, where the principles of ECK can be discussed with visitors from the community in a light, informal way. It is also an event that bonds the ECK initiates together in their appreciation for each other as the awakened lights of the ECK consciousness.

12

When Friends and Family Ask about ECK

12
When Friends and Family Ask about ECK

When people ask, "What is ECKANKAR?" what do I say?

It's best to keep it simple. One answer could be, "It's people trying to learn more about God."

Another possibility is to say that, then ask if the other would like an ECKANKAR brochure. Here's where you must pay close attention. Some people are satisfied with a simple answer. Their eyes or face will say, "Oh!" They'll have just what they need.

Others want more. This second group will like your offer of an ECKANKAR book or brochure.

A good approach is to tell one or two things you like about it. Has it helped you? How?

Above all, give those who ask about ECKANKAR no more than they want. They'd be uncomfortable if they got too much too soon.

A good approach, if they want to know more about ECKANKAR, is to tell one or two things you like about it. Has it helped you? How?

Listen to promptings from the Mahanta for guidance. Keep it simple and light.

How can I explain the Mahanta to my peers?

First, try to determine the level of awareness of the listeners. Do they have a most general, offhand sort of curiosity? Then say the Mahanta's like a teacher or a coach. He tries to show how to live a better life—even as a pastor, priest, or rabbi would.

The Mahanta's like a teacher or a coach. He tries to show how to live a better life—even as a pastor, priest, or rabbi would.

If a questioner persists, ask questions of him on this order: "What religion do you follow?" "How does your pastor (priest or rabbi) try to uplift his church members?"

Listen carefully to the answer. In most cases, you can say, "My spiritual guide does that too."

Let's say that someone is very interested and is ahead of the others in understanding. You may offer that person *Is Life a Random Walk?* or maybe an ECK brochure. Or tell him about the ECKANKAR Web site. This way he can explore it at his own pace.

What if my spouse is not in agreement with my studying ECK?

Concerning situations where the ECK teachings bring a reaction in the home, it is better to step back from the outer works and continue quietly by yourself until matters improve.

You will continue to receive the love and protection of Divine Spirit in spiritual matters as long as you want them.

Divine Spirit tends to hold families together whenever possible. I do not want a husband and wife to fight over their different religious beliefs. Harmony in a family is a sacred thing.

What is the best way to explain the HU to a newcomer?

I think the best way is to say it's a love song to God that can help you. In singing it or holding it in your mind during times of need, it becomes a prayer. It becomes a prayer of the highest sort. It means that we're willing to let the Holy Spirit take care of the affairs in our life according to the divine plan instead of our personal plan.

The HU is a love song to God that can help you open your heart to God's love.

The power of HU can benefit everyone, whether they are Muslim or Christian or of any other belief. It doesn't change one's religion, but it will enhance it.

Let them know that singing *HU* can help open your heart to God's love. Then you may find miracles happening in your life.

How to Find Out More

How to Find Out More

I hope you have enjoyed this brief tour of new opportunities for your spiritual growth and adventure.

The following information, from the ECKANKAR Spiritual Center, on ECK member support, local ECK activities, and additional study aids may answer other questions you have.

The following information may answer other questions you have.

ECK Member Support

ECKANKAR Structure

ECKANKAR is a nonprofit religious organization and church. Within the spiritual direction given by the Living ECK Master, organizational matters at the international level are mainly handled by the ECKANKAR Spiritual Center staff and ECKANKAR Board of Trustees. Affiliated Satsang Societies around the world handle ECKANKAR activities in their regions. The chart on the following page shows some key elements of the ECKANKAR structure.

ECKANKAR Structure

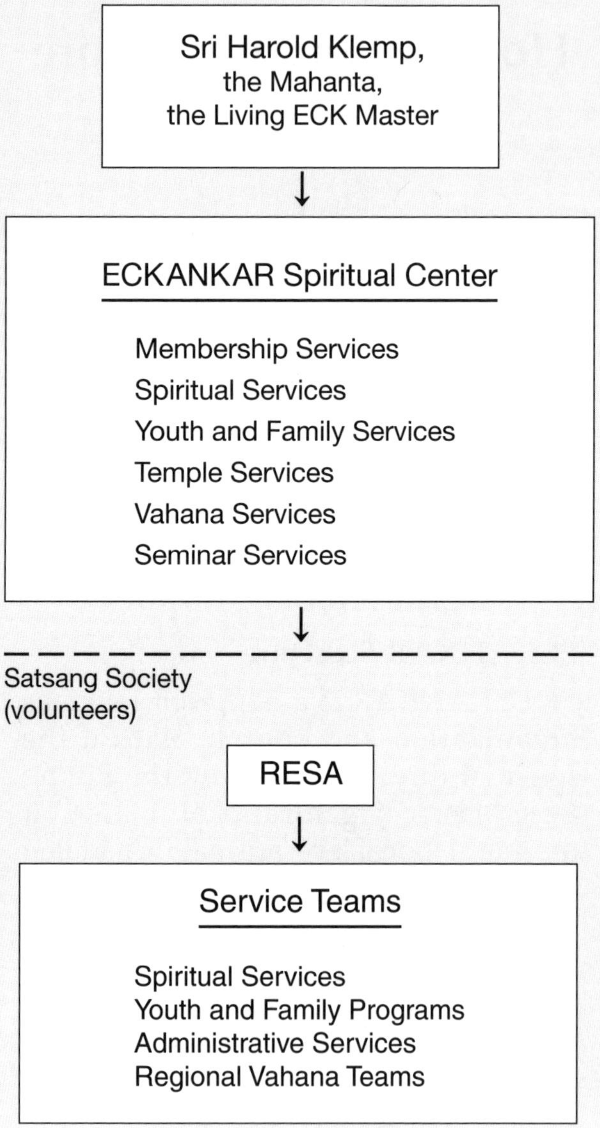

- **The Mahanta, the Living ECK Master**

He is the spiritual leader of ECKANKAR. His duty is to lead Soul back to God. He can assist spiritual students physically as the Outer Master, in the dream state as the Dream Master, and in the spiritual worlds as the Inner Master.

- **ECKANKAR Spiritual Center (ESC)**

At the direction of the Living ECK Master, the ESC brings ECK materials and programs to the world. For example: discourses, books, recordings of the Master's talks, seminars, and the official ECKANKAR Web site.

At the direction of the Living ECK Master, the ESC brings ECK materials and programs to the world.

The Web site offers a large variety of information and services for both ECK members and seekers. It's well worth your time to explore the site and take advantage of all the benefits it has to offer (**www.Eckankar.org**).

See chapter 10 for more about the ESC.

- **Regional ECK Spiritual Aide (RESA)**

A RESA is also an ECK cleric, Initiator, and ESA. He or she is appointed by the Living ECK Master and is his designee to bring the message of the Light and Sound of God to seekers in your country, state, or province. The RESA is responsible for coordinating all ECK activities and volunteers within his or her region. The ECK organization in the region is called the Satsang Society, and its activities include the following service areas:

The RESA is responsible for coordinating all ECK activities and volunteers within his or her region.

- **What Spiritual Services helps you with:**

  ECK classes (including Satsang classes), ECK Worship Services, leadership trainings, initiations, ESA sessions, weddings, memorial services, consecration ceremonies, rites of passage, regional ECK Web sites, and ECK publications.

- **What the youth and family programs help you with:**

  Youth and family activities.

  See chapter 5 to learn more about youth activities.

- **What Administrative Services helps you with:**

  ECK centers, meeting places, and donations which are used for the ECK mission within your region.

- **Ways that regional Vahana (missionary) teams help others find ECK:**

Introductory ECK events, posters, newspaper announcements, TV, etc. Perhaps one of these is how you first discovered and began to explore the ECK teachings.

- **ECK volunteers**

Those who serve in ECKANKAR uphold high spiritual ideals. These ideals are outlined in *Spiritual Duties of the ECK Volunteer*. This document is posted online in the Members Area at the ECKANKAR Web site, **www.Eckankar.org**. (You'll need a copy of the most recent *Mystic World* for the user password, which is always the last word in the title of Sri Harold's lead article.) A printed version of the document is also available.

Those who serve in ECKANKAR uphold high spiritual ideals.

If you'd like to know more about an area of service and don't know the local director, contact your Regional ECK Spiritual Aide (RESA). Let him or her know you are a new ECK member and what you'd like to know more about. "Additional Study Aids," at the back of this book, lets you know how to contact your RESA.

Local ECK Activities

Discover the wonderful opportunities for spiritual growth and fellowship in your region. You are warmly invited to come, join in, and be with other like-minded people on your journey home to God.

- **ECK Satsang classes**

Special classes for ECK members to explore the ECK discourses together. See chapter 4 for details.

- **ECK book discussion classes**

Come share experiences, ask questions, or just listen as the group explores keys to spiritual freedom.

Come share experiences, ask questions, or just listen as the group explores keys to spiritual freedom. These classes are led by a trained ECK teacher (Arahata). Most ECK book discussion classes are open to the public. If yours is, you're welcome to invite friends and family who'd like to know more about the ECK teachings.

The book discussion class may be for adults (those eighteen or older) or for youth (through age seventeen).

- **Roundtables and ECK youth forums**

Roundtables are small group discussions which focus on spiritual topics about the ECK teachings. They are led by ECK

Spiritual Aides (ESAs; see page 64).

ECK youth forums are similar to roundtables but are especially for young ECKists (under eighteen).

- ***Mystic World* and *Letter of Light* discussion classes**

These classes discuss quarterly periodicals from the ECKANKAR Spiritual Center. The parts written by Sri Harold Klemp are the main focus of the class. The *Mystic World* comes with your ECK membership. See page 10 for more.

The *Letter of Light* is a youth newsletter. The discussion class is either for adults (those eighteen or older) or for youth. See page 36 for more.

- **HU Chants**

A HU Chant (or HU Song) is a gathering to sing the ancient love song to God, the HU. It is simply for the spiritual upliftment of those who come and is not directed to any other purpose.

A HU Chant is simply for the spiritual upliftment of those who come.

HU Chants for ECK members only can last up to forty minutes.

The community HU Chant is open to the public and lasts about twenty minutes.

- **ECK Worship Services**

People from all walks of life gather to celebrate a life lived in harmony with Divine Spirit. The ECK Worship Service is for the public and ECK members alike and a great way to introduce friends and family to ECK. Many services include youth programs.

- **ECK regional seminars**

ECK regional seminars bring inspiration and fellowship on your journey home to God.

They are held by ECK members within each region.

Visit the ECKANKAR Web site (**www.Eckankar.org**). Look at "Upcoming Seminars." You'll find a schedule of ECK regional seminars being held around the world.

The creative-arts special interest groups are a way to be trained to carry the message of ECK in certain disciplines.

- **Special interest groups**

The Shariyat-Ki-Sugmad, Book Two, page 247, speaks of the special interests many chelas have when it says, "The initiate gives his services by writing, painting, and other forms of creative arts for and about ECKANKAR. He gains himself while at the same time giving of himself to others through the creative forms."

The creative-arts special interest

groups are a way to be trained to carry the message of ECK and hone your missionary skills in certain disciplines. There are five creative-arts groups:

- ECK Artists
- ECK Film and Television
- ECK Musicians
- ECK Theater
- ECK Writers

The creative-arts groups are for both beginners and those who are more advanced in each discipline. The groups may all sponsor local classes called circles.

The ECK Health Professionals Group offers spiritual insights to licensed health professionals as they pursue their personal mission of service. If you are a health professional and would like to join the group, call or write to the ECKANKAR Spiritual Center to request an application.

All of the special interest groups have annual meetings at the ECK Springtime Seminar.

- **Vahana (missionary) activities**

New members are welcome to join in and support the many ways of sharing the spiritual benefits of the ECK teachings.

New ECK members are welcome to join in and support the many ways of sharing the spiritual benefits of the ECK teachings about the Light and Sound of God.

The Living ECK Master teaches that

We respect the privacy, beliefs, and religious freedom of others.

we have as much to learn from others as to give; that we acknowledge the important spiritual role of other religions and religious leaders; and that we respect the privacy, beliefs, and religious freedom of others.

Do you want to be a part of any of these activities in your region?

If you don't know the local director, call your RESA and let him or her know you are a new ECK member and what you'd like to know more about. "Additional Study Aids," at the back of this book, lets you know how to contact your RESA.

Additional Study Aids

For an at-a-glance overview of the ECKANKAR Spiritual Program, see the chart on page 101.

A Modern Prophet Answers Your Key Questions about Life, Books 1 and 2

Sri Harold Klemp

The Living ECK Master answers hundreds of key questions from people searching for truth and spiritual purpose in their lives.

A Cosmic Sea of Words: The ECKANKAR Lexicon

Sri Harold Klemp

Ultimate companion book for all ECKANKAR literature. An easy-to-use guide to over 1,900 key spiritual terms and concepts.

The Spiritual Exercises of ECK

Sri Harold Klemp

This book is a staircase with 131 steps. But you don't have to climb all the steps to get to the top. Each step is a spiritual exercise, a way to help you explore your inner worlds. And what awaits you at the top? The doorway to spiritual freedom, self-mastery, wisdom, and love.

The Shariyat-Ki-Sugmad, Books One and Two

The Shariyat-Ki-Sugmad, which means "Way of the Eternal," is the holy scriptures of ECKANKAR.

Spiritual Exercises for the Shariyat, Book One

Sri Harold Klemp

Ignite your love and curiosity for the Way of the Eternal in your daily life through contemplation of the Shariyat. These luminous spiritual exercises will unlock the secrets of its beauty and power in your daily life.

Your Road Map to the ECK Teachings: ECKANKAR Study Guide, Volumes 1 and 2

Sri Harold Klemp

A snapshot overview for each item will help you find what you need at any stage of your spiritual journey. It also gives a preview into the ECK discourses for advanced study.

Volume 1 features books by Sri Harold Klemp and Paul Twitchell, as well as general reference and introductory books by other ECK authors. Volume 2 features discourses, tapes, and other writings by Sri Harold Klemp and Paul Twitchell, as well as a wide range of materials for youth.

ECKANKAR Study Materials
(complimentary catalog from ECKANKAR)

Just write or call the ECKANKAR Spiritual Center or request it online.

* * *

Places you can request ECKANKAR study materials mentioned in this booklet.

- Local and online bookstores
- Your local ECK center
  (Contact your RESA or the ECKANKAR Spiritual Center to see if there is an ECK center near you.)
- The ECKANKAR Spiritual Center (mail or phone)
- The ECKANKAR Web site (**www.Eckankar.org**)
- Local public library
  (If they don't have the book, they may be able to acquire it for you.)

Important note:

Youth study materials, audio and video recordings, and certain other items are only available from an ECK center or directly from the ECKANKAR Spiritual Center.

Here's how to contact the ECKANKAR Spiritual Center:

Web-site address

Go online at **www.Eckankar.org**

Phone number

Call (952) 380-2222

Mailing address

ECKANKAR
Attention: Membership Services
PO Box 2000
Chanhassen, Minnesota 55317-2000
USA

Here's how to get in touch with your Regional ECK Spiritual Aide (RESA).

Check your regional ECK Web site or local ECK newsletter. You can also call or write the ECKANKAR Spiritual Center using the above phone number or address and ask for your RESA's contact information.

ECKANKAR
Spiritual Program

Welcome to the Wonderful World of ECK! Your Membership Guidebook book and forums

Karmabusters book and workshop

Spiritual Duties of the ECK Volunteer training

Arahata Training

Be the HU: How to Become a Co-worker with God book and workbook

Handbook for ECK Leaders book and training

The H.I. Letter

Spiritual Duties of the ECK High Initiate training

Wisdom from the Master on Spiritual Leadership: ECK Leader's Guide book, workbook, and training

The Holy Fire of ECK books 1, 2, and 3

Riding for the ECK Brand

Clergy

- Clergy Training
- Initiator Training
- ESA Training

New Member 1 Second Initiation 3 4 Self-Realization 6 7 8 9 10 11 12 God-Realization

- Discourses
- *The Mystic World*
- HU Chants
- Chela Meetings/Workshops

All

- Satsang Classes
- Seminars
- ECK Worship Services
- Four ECK Celebrations of Life

See *Your Road Map to the ECK Teachings: ECKANKAR Study Guide* for a descriptive overview of ECK books, discourses, and recordings.